3/10

HOW TO BE

HOW TO BE
FAMOUS

FAMOUS

★ OUR GUIDE TO LOOKING THE PART, PLAYING THE PRESS, AND BECOMING A TABLOID FIXTURE

HEIDI MONTAG *and* SPENCER PRATT

GRAND CENTRAL
PUBLISHING
New York • Boston

Photos throughout the book appear courtesy of
Pacific Coast News. Used by permission.

Grand Central Publishing
Hachette Book Group
237 Park Avenue
New York, NY 10017

Visit our Web site at www.HachetteBookGroup.com.

Printed in the United States of America

First Edition: November 2009
10 9 8 7 6 5 4 3 2

Grand Central Publishing is a division of Hachette Book Group, Inc.
The Grand Central Publishing name and logo is a trademark of Hachette
Book Group, Inc.

Library of Congress Cataloging-in-Publication Data

Montag, Heidi.
    How to be famous: our guide to looking the part, playing the press, and
    becoming a tabloid fixture / Heidi Montag and Spencer Pratt.—1st ed.
        p. cm.
    ISBN 978-0-446-55591-3
    1. Fame. I. Pratt, Spencer. II. Title.
    BJ1470.5.M67 2009
    306.4'8—dc22   2009015627

Designed by Joel Avirom and Jason Snyder

FROM THE DESK OF SPEIDI

Dear reader,

What you are about to uncover in the pages to come is highly classified and sensitive information. We are writing to you from an undisclosed location (on Robertson Blvd. in Hollywood, of course) and are about to reveal all our most treasured secrets of how we became who we are. Our story contains multiple twists and turns (mostly knives being twisted in people's backs and turns on red carpets, really) and must be followed exactly if you hope to acquire what we have acquired. This material is not for the faint of heart.

　To protect those whose identity we need to conceal at this time (you know, legal stuff) you will not read any references to our show, *The ▮▮▮▮▮▮▮▮▮*. You also will not see the names of some of our closest, um, "friends," Ms. ▮▮▮▮▮▮▮▮, Ms. ▮▮▮▮▮▮, Mr. ▮▮▮▮▮▮, and ESPECIALLY not Ms. ▮▮▮▮▮ ▮▮▮▮▮.

　The information contained in the following pages MUST be handled with the greatest of care. If it falls into the wrong hands, there is no telling what could happen. The last thing we all need are a bunch of people with no discernable talent other than their ability to make themselves famous, running around LA with swarms of paparazzi following their every move. That would be really, really, really awful, wouldn't it? Um, it would, wouldn't it?

　Anyway, forget about that. Just be careful. Do NOT try this at home. And by that we mean: in order to get what you want you have to, you know, go to places other than your home.

　We wish you the best of luck on your mission.

Yours truly,

Heidi & Spencer

Acknowledgments

This book would not have been possible without the help and support of the following people. We'd like to thank Jesus, our families, Nana, Tony Disanto, Adam Devillo, Liz Gately, Van Toffler, Janice Min, Peter M. Grossman, Dan Wakeford, Larry Hackett, Richard Spencer, *TV Guide*, Ryan Seacrest, Perez Hilton, Harvey Levin and TMZ, *Rolling Stone*, Jann Wenner, Jeff Berg, Peter Churnun, David Foster, Barbara Walters, Elizabeth Hasselbeck, Whoopi Goldberg, Joy Behar, David Letterman, Jimmy Kimmel, Conan O'Brien, Jimmy Fallon, Larry King, Ben Silverman, Amanda Ruisi, Rick Rhodes, Mel Berger, Adam Gelvin, Suzie Unger, Lon Rosen, John Fereder, Dan Black, Anne Clark, Ken Burry, The One and Only Palmilla, the paps everywhere, James Aylott, Mike Carrillo and everyone at Pacific Coast News, Mary-Kate Olsen, Kristin Cavalleri, MadeMen baseball, Edward Jones, Wolfgang Puck, Michelle DeLuchs and the staff at Cut, Don Antonio's, Martin Scholler, Matthew Rolston, Hugh Hefner, Todd Moskowitz, Dave Pinsado, Kathy Dennis, Steve Morales, Bill Beasley, Chad Waterbury, King Kevin Casey, Gerardo Mejia, the original Rico Suave, Rickson Gracie, Dr. Frank Ryan, Zoe Rose, and Lincoln Edward Grossman.

CONTENTS

Prologue...1

1 **YOUR POINT OF ENTRY**...5

2 **SPENCER'S GUIDE TO PLAYING THE VILLAIN**...13

3 **HEIDI'S GUIDE TO PLAYING THE BOMBSHELL**...25

4 **PRETTY ON THE OUTSIDE!**...41

5 **THE PAPS ARE YOUR FRIENDS**...51

6 ★ *TELL YOUR STORY*...77

7 ★ *COUPLE POWER!*...89

8 ★ *BUILDING YOUR BRAND*...97

9 ★ *GETTING WORK DONE IS YOUR JOB, BY HEIDI*...105

10 ★ *FAMOUSLY EVER AFTER*...117

Epilogue...127
In Case of Emergency...129

PROLOGUE

You couldn't help it, could you? It's okay. Don't feel guilty. We get it. You probably walked by this in the bookstore and said, "Wait, those #$@%^$# have a BOOK now?" But here you are reading it. Don't hate yourself.

We thought about starting the first page with something like, "Hi, we're Heidi Montag and Spencer Pratt from blah blah blah . . ." or something lame like that. But the point is, you already KNOW that. If you don't know who we are, we can guarantee that your kid does. And that's the point of this book. We're SUPERfamous—and for what? We're on a reality show . . . on cable for that matter . . . and we're not even allowed to acknowledge on the show that our real jobs are, well, being on a reality show!

But why should you listen to us? We're just lucky, right? Just a couple of blond bimbos who like to cause trouble. Well, take a look at this list: Angelina Jolie, Jennifer Aniston, Heath Ledger, Jamie Lynn Spears, Nicole Richie, Jessica Simpson, Suri Cruise, Shiloh Jolie Pitt, Owen Wilson, and Heidi Montag. That's a *Forbes* top ten list of celebrities who have appeared on the most magazine covers in 2008. Everyone else on that list is a long-term A-list star. We're talking Oscar winners, Grammy winners, children of the most famous people on the planet . . . and Heidi. Do you think that happened by accident?

Admit it, you're intrigued. And it's only natural. Because the truth is that whether you love us, hate us, or love to hate us, there IS a recipe for infiltrating Hollywood, and we've got it. Sure, it's not rocket science, but it IS a science. Our expert technique comes from years of careful study of fame and its essential elements, painstaking analysis of its masters, an exhaustive process of trial and error, and, finally, the formulation of the perfect strategy for capturing the attention of the masses.

> **Admit it, you're intrigued. And it's only natural.**

Does that sound serious and articulate to you? Good. Because as airbrushed and airheaded as you may think we are, we're every bit as savvy. But because we're such thoughtful, giving people, we're willing to share. You're welcome.

What you are about to read is our no-fail, no-nonsense (well, some would say it's ALL-nonsense) insider's guide to take you from nobody to notorious. Take it from us, you cannot buy this kind of information. Well, at least you couldn't until now. So go on. What are you waiting for? Hold your head high, march up to that register and shell out the measly $19.99 (aka roughly five *Us Weeklys*.) Next, book your ticket to LA and make sure to tuck this in your carry-on. If you follow our advice, it might just be the last time you ever fly commercial.

> **Take it from us, you cannot buy this kind of information.**

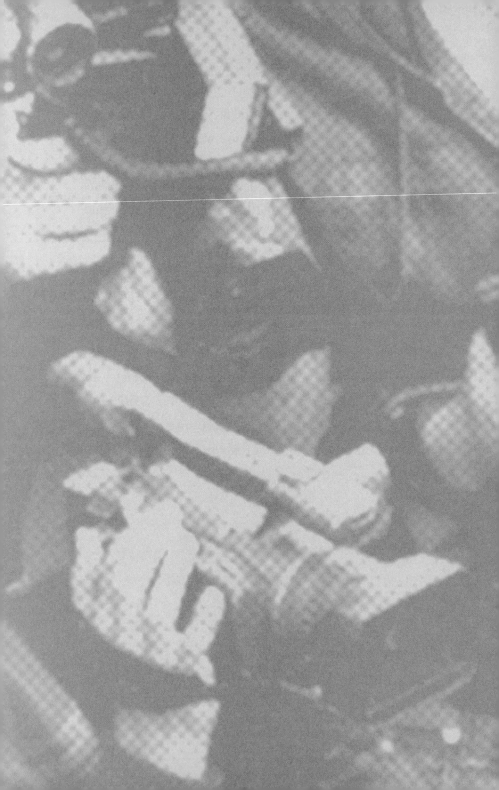

1

YOUR POINT OF ENTRY

We realize this may all seem a bit daunting. We're sure you're sitting there thinking, *How can I possibly get famous? Who am I?* Don't sweat it. Like any problem, there's always a solution. You just need to break it down into steps. You don't just roll out of bed one day and become Madonna or Angelina Jolie. But you'll get there. The first step on your journey is to do something exactly opposite to what you'll be doing once you succeed. Think about other people before yourself. Yes, we know this sounds crazy. Please forgive us for such an outrageous statement. But allow us to explain.

You can't just walk out onto the street and say "Look at me!" and become famous. And unless you're going to do something like crash-landing a plane in the middle of the Hudson River without hurting a single passenger, you're going to have to take a few baby steps. So start by viewing your surroundings. The easiest way to begin your journey to fame is to find an existing group of moderately famous people and join them. Remember, strength in numbers. Hollywood history is littered with famous gangs. From the Rat Pack to the Brat Pack to the Frat Pack, it's always been easier to get famous in a group of people than it is by yourself.

We're no different. Remember, the girls on our show all started out as friends. Let's see, what can we call a bunch of hot chicks running around LA getting famous just for being on TV . . . We'd like to take this opportunity to coin a phrase . . . Ladies and Gentlemen, the Cat Pack. That's what the girls were! Each fell into their roll and played it well: the front woman, the sidekick (Heidi), the vixen, and the fashionista. Now, keep in mind this is only stage one, young grasshoppers. It goes without saying that the eventual goal is to break out and take over. Let's be honest. Today, Heidi

> *It's easier to go farther on a moving train than to start one up yourself.*

is the only one of those girls that can now claim to be a front woman (seven *Us Weekly* covers and counting), a vixen (the only one of them to get her own *Maxim* and *Playboy*

> **You need to take a look at an existing group, figure out what is missing, and fill that void.**

covers), and a fashionista (her clothing line Heidiwood sold out at Kitson in one day . . . twice). That's why WE'RE the ones writing the book! We're the Pratt Pack now, people! But we digress.

Even Heidi had to start somewhere. When she was asked to be on a reality show starring someone who was ALREADY famous for being on a reality show, it was a no-brainer. The lesson again is that it's easier to go farther on a moving train than to start one up yourself. Why go through all the trouble? But you must learn to smile for the camera before you learn to star in your own show, so let's get back to the baby steps.

You need to take a look at an existing group, figure out what is missing, and fill that void. Each gang of celebs has a few essential roles. You've got the leader, the sidekick, the villain, and the role players. Before you introduce yourself to the world, you have to figure out exactly who it is you're introducing. Bear in mind that the public you and the personal private you aren't necessarily the same person—but you'll find it very difficult to keep up a complete façade your entire life, so we recommend staying somewhat close to your natural personality. Whenever our real friends are asked if we're "really like that," they usually say something along the lines of, "Sort of. You're just seeing magnified versions of them on TV." And that's what your persona or character is. A magnified version of yourself.

> ## The problem of starting out as the star is that there is nowhere to go but down.

Now if you're anything like us, you love being the center of attention, and so you figure you should be the star from day one. That's what we thought at first, too. But this is a typical beginner's mistake. Being the Alpha Dog can be very stressful. Sure, every story begins and ends with you, and all the other players in your universe revolve around you like the planets around the sun. And sure, you make the most money, get the best-looking boyfriend or girlfriend, the most publicity, and the best perks. But being the star also means that you will spend the rest of your life having people gunning for your position. You better grow eyes in the back of your head, because there are people out there who can't wait to betray you.

The other problem of starting out as the star is that there is nowhere to go but down. You're constantly playing defense against people vying for your top-dog status, and it's only a matter of time until you're sacked. For these reasons, we suggest you start out as a sidekick. It allows you the chance to build up your character without the pressures of the star so you can plan your next move. Think of it as the minor leagues of celebrity. You're learning the ropes, playing the game, and when you're ready, you get called up to the big leagues. In order to be a sidekick, though, you need to figure out which kind suits you.

There are two basic kinds of successful sidekicks. First you have the Sleeper Sidekick. This is the no-drama mama. To be a Sleeper Sidekick, you basically have to just buddy up with the Alpha Dog and act as a sounding board for everything they say. You'll find yourself doing a lot of nodding and saying things like "Yeah, you're right," "Of COURSE it's their fault," and "I'm so sorry that happened to you." To us, it sounds pretty nauseating, but it CAN be effective. People who

> **There are two basic kinds of successful sidekicks.**

are already famous tend to want to surround themselves with yes people. Obnoxious? Yes. Easy to exploit? Yes again. Pull this off successfully and the general public will look at you as a great friend. They'll think of you rarely, but when they do it will be positive. In our opinion, you are limiting your ceiling for fame if you go this route. It's for people who can't stomach conflict. Sure, it gets you close to the action, but how long can you possibly kiss ass before it really starts to stink? That said, all you have to do is take a look at who the first person to get spun off from our show was and the proof is there. Being the Sleeper Sidekick can take you places.

The infinitely more interesting way to roll is to play the Troublemaker Sidekick. Heidi pulled this off to perfection, of course. The other thing you need to remember about Alpha Dogs is that there are often things that they just can't or won't say or do because they're so worried about saying or doing the right thing all the time. The Troublemaker Sidekick appeals to the Alpha Dog because they can act out in ways the Alpha Dog only wishes they could. As a result, if you play your cards right, you can steal every scene. Remember when

> **The infinitely more interesting way to roll is to play the Troublemaker Sidekick.**

Heidi showed up at that *Teen Vogue* party after she was explicitly told not to? It helped form her character. The Sleeper Sidekick chick NEVER would have pulled that move, but she also never would have gotten her own scene. Establishing the fact that you are your own person early on is a must. Everything you do when you're a sidekick plays off the Alpha Dog, of course, but make sure you are constantly taking things up a notch. You're guaranteed to draw attention to yourself and away from everyone else, and there is no way that can be a bad thing, right? You see, being the number two is actually a great place to be at first. You're visible, but you don't have the responsibilities

> **You're visible, but you don't have the responsibilities of the leader.**

of the leader. You're also a heartbeat away from the top spot. You can straddle the line between servicing the leader and overthrowing them, too. It's a difficult balance to keep, but it's doable.

Of course, there IS another route. You can come in and just be a hurricane of trouble. The Troublemaker Sidekick is a great character to play, but in the end, as long as you are in this role, you're going to have to play second fiddle. But for those who have the stomach to rock it, may we recommend another course of action?

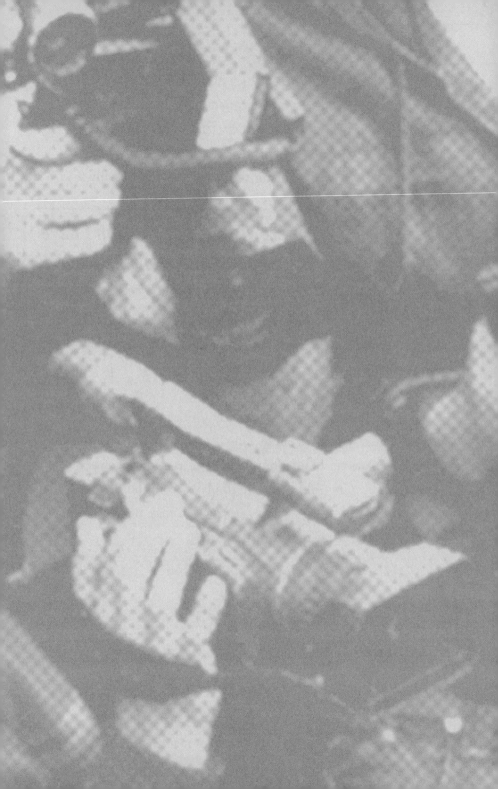

2
SPENCER'S GUIDE TO PLAYING THE VILLAIN

Paul Newman once said, "A man with no enemies is a man with no character." Since Paul Newman is about as famous a Hollywood icon as anyone, what he said must be true. Clearly, I've got more "character" in my left pinky than most people have all over. This is a good thing. My motto is that you shouldn't be afraid to mix it up. The people who you really care about will always be there. The people who get rubbed the wrong way just by you being yourself are not only not worth your time but can make excellent targets. Trust me: there is no greater pleasure on earth than tweaking someone who is just simply asking for it. And the best part is, if you really know what you're doing and choose the right target, you not only get to them, but also everyone watching them at home. Read the user comments on the blogs the next time they do a post about me. It's incredible. Thousands of people I've never met and will never meet waste their time commenting on why they shouldn't be wasting their time talking about me. You think people spend that kind of energy on people they like? All this hating on me does is add fuel to the fire, and they know this. But they STILL can't help themselves! I mean, admit it. Given how the general public feels about me, the chances are that if you're reading this right now, you can't stand me. I get it. If I weren't me, I'd HATE me. But here you are. Now, allow me to elaborate on why and how it's great to be the villain.

If I weren't me, I'd HATE me.

When I was watching pro wrestling growing up, I always rooted for the bad guys. You know why? Because it was really boring watching Hulk Hogan go through the same routine of getting his ass whipped but then somehow finding the strength to pull it out in the end with a body slam and a leg drop. Just like it's really boring watching some blond chick be nice to people, get trampled on by every guy she dates, and end up finding solace in the arms of her friends. Yawn. Think

of a tag team like the Rockers. Everyone liked them, but they were midcard. It was only after Shawn Michaels turned on Marty Jannetty by throwing him through a window that they got REALLY famous. Well, at least Shawn Michaels did. The lesson there, as always, is that it's better to be the bad guy. The other point is that the easiest way to make an enemy is to turn on your friend.

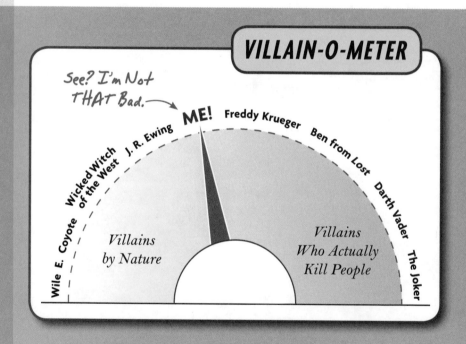

See? I'm Not THAT Bad.

VILLAIN-O-METER

ME!

Freddy Krueger

Ben from Lost

J. R. Ewing

Wicked Witch of the West

Wile E. Coyote

Darth Vader

The Joker

Villains by Nature

Villains Who Actually Kill People

READY!

Of course, my first move in establishing myself as the bad guy was choosing a worthy adversary, and who better than the person who was already the star of the show? Keep in mind that before our current show was even on the air, I had produced a reality show for Fox. Sure, it didn't last long, but even a small show on a broadcast network is bigger than any show on cable. I took a look at our show before I was on it and thought, *What a waste.* That show was about to be canceled. You know why? Because there was NO drama! What were you rooting for? More important, what/who were you rooting *against*? The show needed a steroid boost, and I was just the guy to give it one. Be honest. What's the point of that show starting in its second season if I'm not there? It was fun to come on and be the villain. And hey, I ended up meeting the love of my life! Not too shabby, right?

Now you might think that I picked on someone I didn't like, but where's the fun in that? If you are already at odds with someone there's no story arc, and when creating a feud, the arc is everything. That's why present friends make for the best future enemies. Why bother going through all the trouble of searching for an enemy when the best ones are right there next to you? Or as the legendary Chinese warrior genius Sun Tzu put it: "Know the enemy and know yourself; in a hundred battles you will never peril."

Whether it's Nicole vs. Paris or Heather vs. Denise, it's former friends turned enemies (aka frenemies) that grab instant headlines. That's why when I'm picking a target, no one is off limits. Your best friend. Your own family. Your girlfriend's family. The Olsen twins. The more famous, the better. You may attract more flies with honey, but you attract more fame with bitch slaps.

Eventually, if you build enough tension, not only will people be hanging on your every evil doing, every GOOD deed you do going forward will seem like a much bigger deal until one day, when everyone least expects it, *BOOM*, you can save the day—you know, if you want to wuss out and become a lame good guy, that is. By the way, for those of you who watch the show and are wondering when that moment will happen for me, buy a ventilator because you can't hold your breath that long.

> **When I'm picking a target, no one is off limits.**

AIM!

· ·

Even after you've decided on a target, don't let them know right away. Remember another quote from Sun Tzu: "All war is deception." Learn their weaknesses. This is much easier to accomplish when they still think that you're their friend. The most important thing you can do is to find out the trait that they feel is their most identifiable (we'll call this IT, for "identifiable trait"). For example, are they the "good girl," the "player guy," or the "quiet one"?

To do this, you've got to listen more than you talk (a rare occasion where we would suggest such a strategy). All you are looking for is just ONE skeleton in their closet that goes against their IT. That way you are guaranteed a reaction when you go after them—which, of course, is key. People who would otherwise just say nothing back will go to great lengths to defend themselves when their IT is called into doubt. Shoot for the stars on this one, as the bigger it is, the more mileage you can get from it. That said, don't torture yourself too much by faking a friendship with someone you can't stand for too long. Don't worry; you'll always be able to drum up more on them later.

Now that you've got your hands on something you know is going to drive them nuts, it's time to make your move. Think of it like fishing. Cast your net wide and wait for a bite. Most people can't really help themselves. We all know the right thing to do when someone hurls insults at you just to get attention. Ignore

> **Think of it like fishing. Cast your net wide and wait for a bite.**

them. But believe me, I speak from experience. Someone will respond, and once they do, you've got a full-fledged celebrity feud on your hands! The key is to become increasingly angry at your target.

You must have a short memory . . . when it comes to what YOU'VE said, that is. Treat every attack from your enemy as shockingly unprovoked. It'll help you keep your focus if you're in a constant state of believing that you've done absolutely nothing wrong.

FIRE!

. . . .

It's at this point that we feel the need to pause and remind you that having a conscience is for losers. Don't feel bad. Don't EVER feel bad. Look at them. Just look at the way they [insert their most annoying habit here]. They deserve it. However, if you DO have a conscience, allow me to point something out: being the bad guy doesn't necessarily mean being a "bad" guy. The bad guy's job is just to be opposed to the hero. But let's be honest. A lot of heroes are total tools! Or, even worse, hypocrites. So to give you the best example I possibly can, I'll happily reveal something that I've never revealed before.

I DID IT

. . . .

That's right, I did it. Well, I sort of did it. And don't pretend you don't know what "it" is. If there is one thing that I've been most famously accused of, it is spreading the rumor that my nemesis had a certain piece of video footage of themselves that they'd rather not have become public. Well, guess what? It was me. Now, before I say another word, let me be very clear here. This footage absolutely, 100 percent existed. I didn't make it up. Like I said, I'm not a "bad" guy, I'm just a bad guy. I knew about this for months before I said anything, and I really had no intention of ever talking about it. It sounded like pretty boring footage to me, actually. But when said nemesis attacked Heidi and tried to make her out to be something that she wasn't, well, that was no good with me. So all I had to do was attack my nemesis's IT—in this case, the goody-two-shoes boring-as-vanilla sweetheart. And it wasn't really that hard, actually. The fact that the tape existed had long been reported by *TMZ*. No one really cared, though.

However, when I made a point of reminding every single blog on the planet that it existed, well, let's say it gained traction. I knew it would come back to me. I didn't care. I just couldn't resist tweaking her. See, when you're the villain, you don't have to worry about how your enemy feels.

You can just act out in broad strokes and let the chips fall where they may. And let me tell you it was the smartest thing I ever did. Heidi and I got tied to the story line for good when that happened. The ENTIRE show for the next two years hinged on us vs. her. Sure, there are people who don't like me because of it. But if you care about that, go pick up a copy of *How to Be Liked* by Lamey McLamerson. Fame comes in many shapes and sizes. We're just here to break down your options for you.

3

HEIDI'S GUIDE TO PLAYING THE BOMBSHELL

What can I say? Honestly, I'm one of the nicest people I know. I remember everyone's birthday, I call my mom all the time, I pray every day, and I even let people into my lane when I'm driving on the freeway in LA (no small gesture in Southern Cali!). I've talked about this a million times, but just to be clear, I'm not the bad guy. Seriously, a friend of mine tells me she won't be my friend as long as I stay with the man I love—and somehow I'M the traitor? Three years and a wedding later, you'd think she'd come around, wouldn't you?

But even a small-town sweetie like me can see that there was a huge benefit to playing the bad girl, and I'm not even really a bad girl. It's always better to play a strong role than not play one at all. I'm not going to drop any of those weird Chinese war references on you like Spencer, though. It's really pretty simple. If you find yourself as the sidekick like I did, you really are going to have only two choices when push comes to shove and you want to go out on your own. You either out-nice the good-girl leader of the pack, or turn on her and go your separate way. What sounds more fun to you? Exactly.

> **You either out-nice the good-girl leader of the pack, or turn on her and go your separate way.**

First off, once I realized that I was being looked at as the bitch, I understood that I needed to aim at least one step lower than I thought my opponent would if she were on the attack. I'd never stop reminding people of why my enemy was a loser. If I thought she'd dare make fun of my clothes, I'd be ready and waiting to imply she looked fat in hers. If I thought she'd take a swipe at my man, I'd let people know that hers would rather be with me. And when I couldn't be as goody-two-shoes as her, I'd at least be smarter and funnier. But even while I was sabotaging and smacking down

my opponent, I'd always make sure to present my side as the good girl, just from a different point of view. I'd speak with confidence and conviction so that I'd come across as strong-willed, not just a dumb bitch.

Of course, bona fide bitchiness is not achieved overnight. But if you need to put someone in their place in a pinch, there is one technique that can't fail—and you don't even have to say a word. It's a trick

> *Of course, bona fide bitchiness is not achieved overnight.*

I've developed from playing the reality-show ice princess for so long, and I'd like to share it with you now. Pay close attention here as it's a bit subtle, but if done properly it can be twice as effective as simple yelling. Here you go:

How to Say "I Hate You" Without Saying a Word

by Heidi Montag

Step 1

Exhale deeply, drop your shoulders, and look straight down. This conveys the idea that you've just had a fit of rage, but you've contained it, breathed it out, and controlled yourself. It's also a great setup for what is to come.

Step 2

Turn your head slightly to one side, dart your eyes over to the same side, and gently separate your lips. This tells your target that you're so disgusted by them, you can't even stand to look at them. By moving your head and eyes you've got their attention, but by not making eye contact with them you're giving them the chilly reception they deserve. By opening your mouth ever so slightly, you give the impression that you MIGHT say something that again will have them on the edge of their pathetic seat.

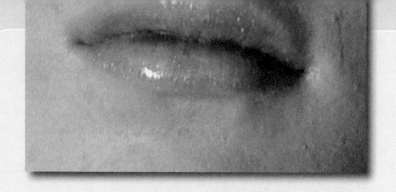

Step 3

Turn your head to the opposite direction, tilt it up slightly, and roll your eyes all the way up to that side. This way your line of sight goes right over theirs. You're basically telling them that you would rather look ANYWHERE— down, left, up, or right—except at their grimy little face. That is, until . . .

Step 4

Repeat Step 1's exhale and shoulder drop, but this time look them square in their beady little eyes. At this point, they've followed your eyes all around the room and will be jarred when you finally stare them down. You've taken

two deep breaths, so you're calm, not frantic, which will definitely disturb them. You've set up the perfect bitch slap without having to lift a finger. Remember, your eyes are the windows to your soul, and they should see as clearly as possible that your soul is about to kick their soul's ass.

There are plenty of reasons why playing the bad girl is the right move. Here are just a few of my favorites:

▶ BITCHES GET THE GUY

Do you think guys fantasize about boring-as-vanilla-ice-cream, cookie-cutter good girls? No way. The nice girl always ends up being the friend or, if a guy is desperate, the friend with benefits. You're way more likely to have someone walk all over you if you're the good girl. Remember, the good girl is the one who gets dumped all the time. And more often than not, she gets dumped for the bitch! How many "Brad left Jen for Angelina" stories do you need to hear to know this? I guarantee every one of you reading this at least knows someone who has been through that scenario. Don't be the Jen. It only leads to heartbreak.

▶ THE CLOTHES ROCK

Definitely one of the perks to being sexy as opposed to just pretty. Think of it like the difference between Anne Hathaway and Angelina Jolie. Who do you think gets more hits on the Internet? Sure, everyone likes to wear jeans, but good girls dress to be comfortable and bad girls dress to be hot. You can be comfortable at home at night when no one is around. But when you go out, whether it's day or night, you want to turn heads. Female villains are always hotter than their good-girl counterparts, so dress the part. Think Sharon Stone in *Basic Instinct*. She was way hotter than the other chick. Catwoman wins out over Rachel Dawes. I'd even take the Wicked Witch over Dorothy so I wouldn't have to wear that silly blue and white dress. You get to show off your body more when you're the bad girl, so rock it. Rest assured, you're never going to see ME in a maxi dress!

▶ YOU'RE MORE MEMORABLE

Quick, name the female star of the first *Beverly Hills 90210* show. I bet you said Shannon Doherty's Brenda, didn't you? You know why? Because Shannon Doherty was a badass, that's why! She came out of that show with the biggest buzz because of her status as a bad girl. You just get more attention when you're the bad girl because people just assume women to be good. There are WAY more villains that are men, so you'll stand out even among villains just for being a chick. There's only one Catwoman amongst the Joker and Two-Face and the Riddler and the Penguin and so on. Simple supply and demand here, people.

STAND BY YOUR MAN

One thing that I can definitely recommend that may seem a bit counterintuitive is that you should always stand by your man. This will be easy if you're both playing the bad guys, of course. If he's a soft wuss, feel free to ditch him. I know it might sound chauvinistic, but a guy can be a bad boy and still be looked at positively (women love their bad boys, don't they?) but a woman can have the pitfall of being JUST a bitch, which is okay when dealing with men but bad news for you if you're trying to market anything to women later on. Remember, you're going to try to sell clothing lines and perfume and shoes, so you do have to remain somewhat likable to women. Moms are going to have to let their teenage daughters buy your stuff, so you have to be one stop beneath a male villain on the hate-o-meter. Standing by your man is a redeeming quality in a woman that makes you more sympathetic. Love softens everything.

TEARS: WWMD (Woman's Weapons of Mass Destruction)

· ·

Now you may be worried about coming across too hard if you're always the bad girl, but as a woman you can soften yourself at any time. Of course, one distinct advantage you have going for you more than anything else is the fact that you can always cry. A crying woman trumps all things. C'mon, ladies, you've tried it at home, you know. I'm not saying it's actually possible, but let's pretend for one second that you MIGHT be wrong in an argument one day. Just go to the waterworks and all is forgiven, isn't it? It's biological. Men and women alike respond to a crying woman with extreme sympathy. Even the most hardened villainess can break people down with puppy-dog eyes and a few tears.

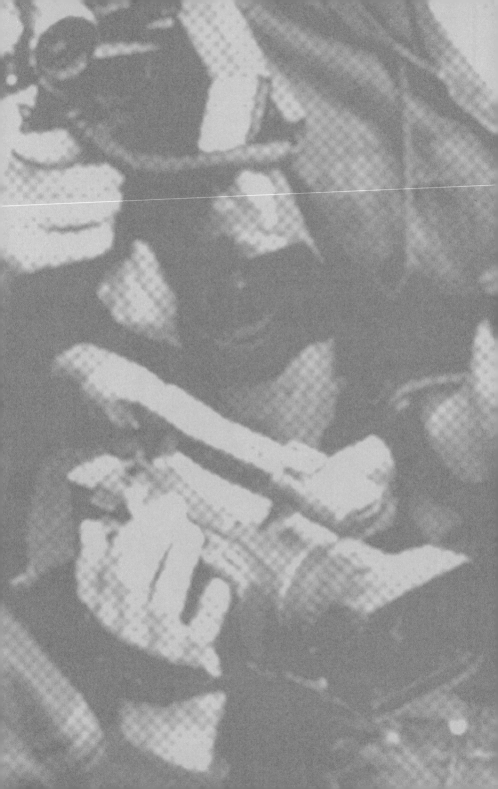

4

PRETTY ON THE OUTSIDE!

There is no reason to sugarcoat it. If you want to be famous, you have to look the part. We're not here to talk about whether or not that's fair. We're here to tell you that you need to get used to the idea of looking good for a living. Honestly, there is no excuse not to. You're a celebrity. It's your JOB to look good. There's no reason you shouldn't be hot. It's not like you're working or anything! For our money, Jennifer Aniston has the hottest body in Hollywood. It was revealed in a magazine cover that during a Cabo vacation over New Year's, she woke up early for a six a.m. jog on the beach every day. Now, some people might think that's a bit excessive. She's on vacation, she should sleep in and enjoy herself, right? To that we ask: on vacation from WHAT, exactly? OF COURSE she's running on the beach at six every morning. She wouldn't be doing her job if she wasn't! Would you tell a policeman not to go to the shooting range, or a teacher not to study her lesson plan, or a baseball player not to take batting practice? Celebrities' commitment to physical perfection is no different. We can't possibly stress this enough. There is no universe in which you should let yourself go physically.

So what are you going to do? Maybe you're Gisele Bündchen and you were just born perfect. If so, you can skip the rest of this chapter. If not, listen up.

FITNESS

First of all, you should want to be fit. Physical fitness, or the lack of it, actually is a huge problem in this country. You'll just feel better about yourself, be happier, live longer, blah, blah, blah. But hey, we understand. This isn't a "feel good about yourself" book; it's a "get famous" book. So here's the real reason you need to be in shape: the weeklies care! Sure, the biggest stories for tabloids are weddings. But there isn't always a coverworthy hookup or breakup or rehab stint, and at times like those the mags turn to diet and fitness stories. And you know what? They sell through the roof. Whether it's Jessica Simpson's yo-yo body, Carnie Wilson or Oprah Winfrey's EXTREME yo-yo bodies, or just how to look hot like Jennifer Aniston, the magazines turn to cover stories about diets and getting in shape as an easy way to score a huge sale without any news to sell off of. This is especially true around the holidays as everyone stuffs themselves from Thanksgiving through New Year's, suddenly looks in the mirror, and realizes they've put on ten pounds in cranberry sauce alone. This past Christmas/New Year's *Us Weekly* did THREE body covers in a row! Believe us when we say that they wouldn't be banging those out one after the other after the other if they weren't continuing to sell. The two highest-selling covers in the history of *Us Weekly* are Jessica

Simpson losing twenty pounds in two months and Heidi's interview about calling off our engagement.

This should tell you two things. One is that you should listen up when the person with the highest-selling cover in the history of *Us Weekly* is giving you advice on how to get famous, and the other is that diet/weight-loss stories are HUGE in the tabloids.

If you put in the work and have a slamming body, the magazines will come calling. One of the first magazine stories we ever got on was a "getting in shape" story; *Us Weekly* came to the gym with us, and we went through our workout with them and revealed our stay-fit secrets. Of course, if we had been revealing all our secrets it would have gone something like, "Uh. We're celebrities now. We have a private chef who steams our vegetables, a personal trainer who comes to our house to bust our asses seven days a week, and enough money to have every conceivable procedure done in case we need a little assistance from time to time." However, since that would have made for quite a short story, we kept that get-fit secret to ourselves. And listen, it *is* hard work. Celebrities are there to look hot for the common people. It's our job. The only problem is when you run into someone who actually takes themselves seriously, as though what they were doing as a celebrity was somehow important. We're just dessert, that's all. We can't really eat a lot of dessert, but we're not important beyond providing a little fun and distraction to everyday people. That being said, if you want to fit in among the rest of us in Hollywood, you have to look the part. Here are some tips:

Work out—constantly. Heidi never stops busting it. She'll be sitting on the couch, just hanging out with friends and lifting her knees up to do crunches while she talks. Spencer boxes, plays squash three times a week, and runs on the treadmill while taking business calls. Don't get lazy. Most people find it easier to work out with a trainer. Sure, it can be expensive, but think of it as an investment in your greatest asset—your appearance! It's just easier to keep going when you've got someone else to answer to who will keep you from going easy on yourself. Of course, as you should be thinking with all things, feel free to work out somewhere you can be seen.

> **Celebrities are there to look hot for the common people.**

It always makes for a great pap picture when you can be seen doing your workout. Yoga in the park, running through the neighborhood, or just getting on the treadmill closest to the window at the gym will all do the trick. (NOTE: THIS is why celebrities wear makeup to the gym!)

STYLE

· ·

Now that you've got your smoking bod, don't stop there. Get thee to a stylist, because the clothes you wear are equally important to how you look. Think of a stylist as a personal trainer for your outfit. If you don't believe us, just take a look at Heidi's wardrobe during the first season on our show compared to what she wears today. Her look went from cute girl next door to hot fashionista, and while she's always had a great sense of style, her stylist whipped her into shape. Plus, once the fashion world started recognizing Heidi as a fashion plate, they started giving her clothing for free because they wanted her to be seen wearing their stuff in public. She's even had her own fashion line! Seriously, people probably don't know the extent to which celebrities live for free. It's bizarre. The more money you make, the less stuff you have to pay for. Incredible, right? Anyway, the lesson here is work the connections and never wear anything less than hot, new, and divaworthy.

Also, remember to accessorize. Bags are massively important, right up there with shoes. Magazines do whole spreads just on people's bags! Choose your stuff wisely, as you'll be judged harshly, but one way or another, make sure to make a statement with your accessories.

HAIR. MAKEUP. NAILS.

. . . .

Obviously, they should ALWAYS be done. You're going to have your picture taken at all times, so do not EVER leave the house without being 100 percent groomed. We find that the best thing to do is just pretend that the second you walk out your door, you're stepping onto a red carpet. You don't want to be that person who gets papped in sweats, no makeup, and a ponytail taking your garbage out, and neither do we! That's why we're vigilant about our appearances at all times. They're Just Like Us: They pump their own gas! = good thing. They're Just Like Us: They look terrible when they wake up in the morning! = bad thing. Bottom line, look the part. If you want to be cast as a celebrity, you better look like one. Plus, you never know when you're going to get the urge to frolic on the beach in a bikini, and just in case the paps are there—and if you're lucky, they will be—you'll want to make sure you look your best.

5

THE PAPS ARE YOUR FRIENDS

Some celebs get it and some just don't. But we're here to tell you that the paps are your friends. For anyone seeking fame, the paparazzi are your most indispensable ally. You don't just want them to follow you. You NEED them to follow you! And the thing is, they WANT to do it! The existence of paps is without question the single biggest thing you have going for you in the fame game. Think about it. It is someone's JOB to follow you around, take your picture, and then sell those pictures to magazines to make you more famous! What other profession in the world has an army of people working for their cause that they don't have to actually employ? Just LOOK at that picture. That's us walking

down Robertson Blvd. There were probably twenty guys following us around that day while we just had lunch and shopped. And every one of them was desperate to help us get our picture into the tabloids. How can this possibly be a bad thing? Of course, some celebs are completely ungrateful, especially after they've made it. We find these people embarrassments to the industry.

PAPARAZZI 101

· ·

So let's get this straight. You want to be a star. You want all
the perks of being famous. You want to not have to wait in
line at the airport, to get a table at any restaurant in town.
Oh, and let's not forget, not actually have to WORK for a
living! And on your way up, you do whatever it takes . . . but
once you get a little taste, you suddenly turn on the forces
that got you there in the first place? Isn't that like a dude
pulling out every stop to get a girl—flowers, little love notes,
fancy dinners—and then, once he sleeps with her, dumping
her? How do we feel about guys who do this? Well, that's
what we think of people who don't get that the paps are your
friends. Do not become one of these people. It's the first sign
that you're taking yourself too seriously, and that will eventually lead to your downfall.

Guess what the best way to NOT get into the magazine is? That's right, don't have your picture taken! Without that, you don't even have a chance. Getting papped is definitely a bit weird at first. You have to get used to flashes and being startled by people showing up out of nowhere and pointing cameras in your face. The first time we got papped, we were at one of our favorite restaurants, Don Antonio's. We ate there all the time on our show, and paps just figured out they could hang out there and we'd eventually show up. We walked outside and there was this explosion of bright light and people yelling our names. Believe it or not, our first instinct was to cover our faces, but we figured out after about 2.3 seconds that these guys were actually on OUR side! We're after fame; these guys are just here to help facilitate it. Sure it takes away some of your private space, but trust us, once you see yourself in the magazines a few times, you'll gladly make that trade. So here are some ways to make sure that the paps find you and stay interested enough in you to keep sending shots of you to the mags:

GO TO THEM

They're not coming to you, at least not at first. There are some go-to spots where the paps always are. Frequent them. In LA, you can't go into the Ivy without having your picture taken. It's where people go *to* have their picture taken. Anywhere on Robertson Blvd. will do as well—celebs love to shop!

There are literally more photographers there than actual shoppers. You can't miss them. More important, they can't miss you. We always make a point of hitting up Robertson if we haven't had our picture taken in awhile. It's a go-to spot. Also, keep tabs on which club is the current hot spot in Hollywood. It changes more often than Paris changes boyfriends, so stay up-to-date.

In New York, SoHo is key. Paps always surround all the shops on Broadway by Prince or Spring Street, or the bars at the big hotels like the Soho Grand or the Mercer. It's not quite Robertson Blvd., but New York is not quite LA when it comes to paparazzi and fame, either.

And as an aside, let us just say one more time for the record that this is information that celebrities are completely aware of. If they wanted to avoid the paps, they absolutely could. So anyone who walks down Robertson wearing a miniskirt who later complains about her privacy is either a liar or an idiot—perhaps both.

BE FRIENDLY

Remember, the paps are just doing their jobs, and contrary to what you may have heard, they're not looking for a fight. These guys, especially the ones who are hanging out in the obvious places, aren't there to work too hard for the picture. Be accommodating. For instance, we always take a minute

to stop and smile, wave, give the peace sign, whatever. If we're together, we always give them a kiss picture. We also make sure to face every direction. This is especially important because people at magazines often want to use pictures where a celebrity is facing a certain way. Never leave it to chance.

Take a second to look at your surroundings and, if possible, incorporate them. Is it the holiday season? Find a guy dressed as Santa Claus and sit on his lap. Anything you can use to make the picture a bit more interesting makes it more likely to be used. There are rare instances in which a train wreck of a picture (for example, people running from the paps, covering up, etc.) will run in a magazine, but for the most part magazines want to see you smile. Don't cover your face—unless you're really ugly, and if you are, you may want to skip ahead to the plastic surgery chapter.

WEAR BRIGHT COLORS

You'd be shocked at how many pictures make it into magazines purely because of the colors in them. Unless you're Marilyn Manson, stay away from black. Magazine editors want their pages to look pretty, so give them a hand.

LOSE THE SHADES

Yes, we know how cool you are. The sun shines on you twenty-four hours a day. We get it. But you're three times more likely to get your picture into a magazine if your eyes aren't covered up. Remember, you're not a Secret Service agent hiding in the bushes. You want you—and as much of you as possible—to be seen at all times.

A quick word on lighting, if we may. When a star appears in a movie or on a television show, or even in an interview on a talk show, a great deal of effort goes into them being lit properly to look their absolute best. The same goes for photo shoots, of course. There are people whose JOB it is in all of those settings to check on the lighting. But when you're having your impromptu photo shoot, courtesy of the paps, you have only yourself to take care of these things.

That being said, learn about the sun. There are certain times of day when you just don't want your picture taken. The first is high noon, when the sun is its brightest. You're guaranteed to be squinting (as we've already established that you should NOT be wearing sunglasses), and since the light is that bright, you just look pale. The other time, for the most part, is at night. Now we know what you're saying: you have to go out at night in order to be seen, right? Sure, showing up at clubs helps. But when your picture is taken at night, they're going to use flashes—and paps aren't dealing in the high-end, flattering strobes that you see at photo shoots. It's going to be very harsh lighting, and there's almost no way you can look good that way. That's why we almost never go out at night.

YOUR TIME TO SHINE

NOON

10 am | 2 pm

8 am | 4 pm

TOO BRIGHT!
*Harsh Lighting =
Bad Pictures*

*Nice light, but are
you really getting
up this early?*

6 am

6 pm

MAGIC HOUR!

You want to go for what we call magic hour: either early in the morning or during the couple of hours before the sun sets. Take our word for it, this is when EVERYONE looks their best. There's a reason we always look so good in our beach shots. Obviously it helps if you go to beaches like Santa Monica where the paps are always hanging around, but keep in mind that they're there all day. Only go when you'll look your best. You're the celebrity. They're on *your* clock!

PAPARAZZI 101, PART DEUX

If you've been following closely so far, you should be some-what famous by now. After a while, the same old pictures of you shopping at Kitson or eating lunch will all start to blend together in the eyes of magazine editors and their readers. It's up to you to kick it up a notch. The last thing you want to be is boring, right? There are many ways of upping the ante, and the paps will love to come along for the ride with you.

LOCATION, LOCATION, LOCATION

The key to real estate and pap pictures is location. You're going to need to travel in order to make the pictures of you more interesting. Obviously, this isn't something that will work before you're famous, as the paps won't make the ef-fort to follow you out of town until they've been able to sell your pictures once or twice. But now that you've established yourself, it's time to branch out.

A quick note: if a celebrity goes on vacation, but there are no paps there to photograph it, did they really go? In your case, you might as well not have. If you've followed our advice, you've realized that the paps are your friends, and you've probably established a rapport with them. This is a good thing in every way. They'll give you your space when you need it if you give them the pictures when they need them. Simple as that.

Considering this, you just need to give a friendly tip to one of the guys shooting you that you're going away for the weekend and you can't wait, etc. Drop the name of the resort, look at them and smile, and they will get it. Nothing gets a pap's juices flowing like a chance to get an exclusive set of pictures out of town. Now that you have that sorted, pack your bags!

Start small. The key is to head somewhere that doesn't look like LA. Head up to Santa Barbara or out to Palm Springs. There are great resorts in both areas, and they're picturesque enough that they'll make for great photos. ALWAYS think in terms of how a magazine will present the pictures. One picture in a magazine is great, but if you can spin it into a STORY, that's when you get multiple pages. If you're in a couple, think, "Their Romantic Getaway." Make sure that you give up a wide vari-

ety of pictures. Lay out by the pool in your bathing suits. Go out to dinner. Partake in any kind of activities you can (horseback riding, golfing, bike riding, etc.).

Remember, the more diverse the pictures are, the more pages you'll be able to get out of it.

Make sure you really give it up, as well. Interact with your partner. Hold hands, kiss, go for long walks on the beach,

play in the pool, and gaze lovingly at one another. You've been reading the tabloids for years, I'm sure. Imagine what you'd want to see in there and act it out for the camera.

If you're single, turn your time away into a girls' or guys' weekend. The same rules apply. Just make sure that you set up enough moments that it conveys a fun trip. Remember, the tabloids are your own personal photo albums. Fill them up with fun stuff!

CELEBRATE GOOD TIMES, COME ON!

You need to treat every special occasion like a red-carpet event. Pay attention to the calendar. Magazines are always doing themed pages, and like anyone else, they love it when other people make their jobs easier. Do them that favor and play right into it. There are

some go-to spots at various times of the year that you'll need to hit up. If it's October, you need to hit Mr. Bones Pumpkin Patch in LA. There are paps stationed there every weekend leading up to Halloween. And of course, when Halloween itself rolls around, make sure that your costume stands out. At Thanksgiving, make sure that you're at a soup kitchen or a place like the Mission in LA, serving food to the less fortunate. Good for your soul *and* for raising your profile. Everybody wins!

Christmastime offers up a ton of photo opportunities. You can have your picture taken shopping for presents

for your significant other. You can get papped picking out your Christmas tree. And just about every street corner gives you the chance to get the classic shot of you sitting on Santa's lap. 'Tis the season to get your picture taken, people!

Do it up on Valentine's Day with your significant other. We want to see roses, new jewelry, chocolates, the whole thing. Make your audience feel like they were there on your date with you. Wear green on St. Patrick's Day. Go on an Easter egg hunt and hang with the Easter Bunny. Take your mother out on Mother's Day. Be patriotic on the Fourth of July. These are all easy ways to get yourself into the pages of the tabloids. Holidays are a gift. Take advantage of them all.

YOUR LIFE, IN PICTURES

The paps are a wonderful tool you can use to advance your own story line. There are times when a picture is worth more than a thousand words. It can often be way more effective to SHOW what's going on in your life rather than just talk about it. It also adds a little juice to your story if people feel like they're seeing something they weren't supposed to see. For example, if you're a couple who has been together for a while, you don't necessarily need to give out quotes on the possibility of getting engaged. All the guy has to do is get photographed in a jewelry store looking at rings. It's like you're taking your fans shopping with you! If you're married, you don't have to give an interview about wanting kids. Just have your picture taken going into a Baby Gap or Kitson Kids. Be sure to hold up the clothes in the air for the pictures—and guys, make sure to rub your woman's belly at all times. The speculation stories alone will carry you for months! If you're about to break up, go out without your wedding ring on, or hang out with another member of the opposite sex. Then people won't just hear rumors, they'll have a visual aid to get them more into what's going on in your life. Remember: quantity + variety = coverage. There are WAY more paps and celebrities/celebrity wannabes out there than there are pages in the tabloids, so make every shot count!

6

TELL YOUR STORY

Now that you've nabbed the spotlight, it might be tempting to coast for a little while. But remember, everyone is replaceable to some degree. If you fail to continue to churn out the drama that got people interested in the first place, you're doomed to never see your sixteenth minute. Never lose sight of the fact that there are always people who legitimately want you to go away. It's like any career, really. There's always someone beneath you who wants your job. If you're the starting quarterback for the Cowboys, the backup wants your job. If you're the manager of a McDonald's, the assistant manager wants your job. And if you're a celebrity, there are people out there who want to take your spotlight.

There's a limited amount of attention to go around. So it is vitally important that you do everything in your power to speak early and often, making sure that whatever you're serving up is nice and juicy!

Remember that it doesn't always have to be positive attention you're bringing to yourself. The idea that there's no such thing as bad press is a cliché, but it became a cliché for a reason. It's totally true! Take, for example, the first video Heidi put out. It was for her song "Higher," and at the time no one even knew Heidi wanted to be a singer. She had this

> **Remember that it doesn't always have to be positive attention you're bringing to yourself.**

song that was okay but not great, and we didn't have any record label or real producing/songwriting/managing team for her, the way someone like Britney Spears does (or that we actually have for Heidi now). But we had this song, and our options were limited. We could have spent what little money we had at the time and tried to make a legit music video. But we all know that would have been awful. People would have seen it once and been bored by it and moved on. No one really would have noticed. Instead, we decided to stay true to our characters and do something completely ridiculous—and 100 percent visible.

PROFESSIONAL AMATEURS

You saw it. You know you saw it. You probably watched it about five hundred times on usmagazine.com—admit it! For the three of you out there who didn't, we'll explain. We took a boom box and Spencer's video camera to a beach where we knew the paps would catch us. Spencer then played the song over and over again on the stereo while Heidi frolicked around, looking hot in her bikini. Was it ghetto? Ghetto fabulous, maybe. But were people talking about us for weeks? You're damn right they were! See, if we had put out something pro, it would have been swept under the rug. But by going over the top in every single way (and really, when do we NOT do that?) and making it as low-budget as possible, we got the best free press you could hope for! We weren't putting it out there so people could debate whether or not it was good. We KNOW it wasn't good. That wasn't the point. The point was to get people talking—and that certainly happened, didn't it? All of a sudden, whether you thought about her in a good way or a bad way, you were thinking about Heidi; you knew she was an aspiring singer. We had multiple follow-up stories to tell about how "humiliated" she was by the reaction that she, of course, KNEW was coming.

A Cautionary Tale

Now, we believe it's important here to include a cautionary tale that illustrates the risk of NOT taking control of your story and instead just going with the flow and hoping that you get taken care of by your friends in the media. We're here to tell you that it won't happen. Here's an example we think you may be familiar with that will bring our point home.

Let's say you're a reality star on a hit show. You're a beautiful, fun-loving girl who has a bad-boy boyfriend. People like you because you're the main star's sidekick and you're pretty and they feel bad for you because you're always getting jerked around by your man. Well, let's say that one day you hear that despite the fact that she has a squeaky-clean image and is always talking smack about him, this best friend hooks up with your boyfriend. Obviously, you're devastated.

However, once the tears have dried the sidekick sees an opportunity. If you're a smart sidekick, your next move is simple. As word starts to leak out that this unthinkable betrayal has occurred, you make a very general statement about how you're just working through some things. Then, when the buzz hits a fever pitch, *BAM*! You give the tearful tell-all. It practically writes itself, doesn't it? "Betrayed By My Best Friend: How she stabbed me in the back and lied about it." That's a guaranteed magazine cover, isn't it? What person isn't going to feel horrible for you and be disgusted by your traitor EX–best friend? At this point you're on the road to totally flipping the script and becoming the beloved new star and banishing your now frenemy to loser status.

Of course, there's only one way to mess things up and not take advantage of such a golden opportunity. How? We'll tell you how. In this case, the sidekick made the mistake of just sitting back and saying nothing and hoping that the other person would just miraculously look bad. And this failure to act in her own best interest cost her her once-in-a-lifetime chance at true stardom, leaving her to languish in what we call Sidekick Purgatory. Call it bad management. Call it low self-esteem. Whatever you do, don't let Sidekick Purgatory happen to you!

SPIN CITY

The finest example of our storytelling skills would have to be Heidi's *Us Weekly* cover interview about her plastic surgery. We'll get into it in more detail a bit later, but the basic idea here is that if you're doing your job right, people are going to be talking about you. If you're REALLY doing your job right, they'll be talking about you the way YOU want them to talk about you. When you get plastic surgery, people notice. If Heidi had just sat back, not commented on it, and let the pictures speak for themselves, people would have walked all over her and given her grief for not coming clean. But because she sat down and spilled her guts about why she did it, she came across as sympathetic. The cover line was even "Revenge Plastic Surgery"! Instead of being just another Hollywood girl with implants, Heidi became a sweet, emotional girl who had always not felt as good about her body as she did about herself and took action to feel better. Now, Heidi actually IS a sweet, emotional girl, but if she hadn't talked about it and actually shown the world who she was, the story would have controlled her instead of the other way around. The additional lesson here, of course, is that in the idea of controlling your story, the key word there is *story*. Anything that gives you a reason to talk about yourself can only be a good thing. And while Heidi played that hand as well as it could have been played, we must of course bow down before the masters.

THE GOLD STANDARD

. . . .

It should come as no surprise to you that the undisputed king and queen of image control are Brad Pitt and Angelina Jolie. And before you say, "Well, they just hired good publicists," you should know that Angelina Jolie has NEVER had a publicist and Brad hasn't really had one since he's been with her. When Brad dumped Jennifer Aniston for Angelina Jolie, all hell should have broken loose. This is a guy who often plays romantic leads in movies he wants women to go see. It SHOULD have been a crushing blow to his career to bail on girl-next-door Jen for home-wrecking head case Angelina.

But Brad is no dummy. Even before he and Jen formally split, he started playing up the kid angle. He was literally teary-eyed during one interview with the *Ocean's Eleven* guys, talking about how all he wanted was to be a dad and that it was the only thing that mattered to him. George Clooney had to change the subject to save him! Now THAT'S controlling your story line.

Sometimes you have to think about these things even before crisis strikes. When Brad and Jen split, the story SHOULD have been all about how he dumped her for Angelina. And while that was part of it, right alongside the cheating speculation was the idea that Jen just didn't want to give him a kid and she only wanted to work on her career. What was poor Brad to do? Hey, didn't he just say that all he ever wanted was children? What a sweetheart. What kind of woman WOULDN'T want to give Brad Pitt a baby, anyway? Angelina wasn't the vixen anymore; she was the mother figure.

And just in case you didn't get the point, a few months after the split, Brad set up an eighty-page photo shoot with *W* magazine with him and Angelina playing the parents of a bunch of young children. They even called it Domestic Bliss! The ink wasn't even dry on the divorce papers, and he's playing house with the woman he left his wife for! But what could you say? EVERYONE was dying to see those pictures because they all just wanted to see

We salute you, Mr. Pitt!

Brad happy as a father. Jennifer Aniston even said at the time that the shoot showed Brad was missing a "sensitivity chip," but she had it all wrong. He has the "telling my story MY way" chip, and we should all learn a lesson from that.

It's 2009, and all three parties are STILL keeping the story going by commenting on it in all their interviews, but the clear winner here is Brad. There literally is not another situation in the history of Hollywood where a man left a woman as beloved as Jennifer Aniston for someone like Angelina Jolie and STILL ended up as the good guy. We salute you, Mr. Pitt!

COUPLE POWER!

*All I need in this life of sin,
is me and my girlfriend.*

—JAY-Z

Especially if that girlfriend is really famous like Beyoncé, right? If there is one thing we've learned, it's that celebrity relationships can put you on the fast track to fame. Think about it—the weeklies are always broadcasting some kind of hookup or breakup, lovefest or heartbreak. "Crazy in Love," "Ready to Wed," "On the Rocks," "It's Over"—you've heard all of these lines before. And it's what keeps us all coming back for more! Given the built-in publicity hook celeb coupledom provides, it shouldn't come as a surprise that we work the relationship angle to the fullest extent. Now don't get us wrong—we couldn't be more in love. But we can't deny the fact that our love is mutually beneficial in more ways than one. And why should we? Our relationship basically IS our job, right? That's what we do for a living. We're a couple. The simple fact is that Speidi > Spencer + Heidi. Hey—we don't make the rules, we just choose to work them to our advantage. Don't believe us? It's true, we're just one example of a time-tested law of celebrity math:

$$C \text{ LISTER} + C \text{ LISTER} = B \text{ LISTER}$$
$$B \text{ LISTER} + B \text{ LISTER} = A \text{ LISTER}$$
$$A \text{ LISTER} + A \text{ LISTER} = A+ \text{ LISTER!}$$

This law holds from the bottom to the top of the celebrity world. Vanessa Minnillo and Nick Lachey on their own? Meh. Put them together and they're hot enough to make the tabloids. Now look at Beyoncé and Jay-Z. One's a major singer/actress, and the other's a big-time rapper and entrepreneur. But couple them up and they're larger than life! Don't even get us started on Tom and Katie, or Brad and Angelina! It works at every level. The whole is greater than the celebrity parts.

Now, if there is one thing you have to remember, it is that when you're famous, especially if you're still TRYING to get famous, there is no such thing as a personal life. You want privacy, be a hermit. You want to be a star? Well, then, you're going to count on your audience for your livelihood, and we're going to have to get to know you, and that means everything about your love life. You tell your sister about the guy you're seeing, don't you? You tell your buddies about the girl you hooked up with last night, right? Well we expect the same access to you. The sooner you figure this out, the better. It's sad to watch some celebrities think that they somehow deserve some sort of privacy that they know full well they'll never have. The more you fight this the less people will like you, and you'll wake up one day and realize no one cares anymore, and you'll be embarrassed to have to crawl back and dish in hopes of a second chance. EVERYBODY talks about their relationships! Don't be a tool. If Brad, Angelina, and Jennifer can still talk about how Jen got screwed and how Brangelina are living happily ever after in EVERY magazine interview they give to this day (and don't think that's by accident), so can you.

Now that you're mentally prepared to make your love life the stuff of gossip magazines, we're here to tell you that if you follow some simple guidelines, you'll get through this just fine.

LOUD AND SHAMELESS

Remember that every little fight with the person you're dating should become a headline. There are various stages of breakup, just like there are various stages of a romantic relationship. Each one of them should be out in the open to guarantee as much publicity as possible. We're no different. We've gone through quite a bit in the years we've been together, but being open and accessible about it has been great for us. Again, communicating with your audience is key to them caring about you and your story line. People may love us or hate us, but because of our openness and honesty, they know everything there is to know about us and can follow our story more easily. Never underestimate the importance of making things easy for your audience. We like easy. We like air-conditioning and pictures in our books and seats that recline. Make your story the EZ Chair of the celebrity world.

TABLOID RELATIONSHIP STATUS-O-METER

Ready to Wed!
. . . .

Crazy in Love!
. . . .

It's Getting Hot!
. . . .

It's On!
. . . .

On the Rocks!
. . . .

It's Over!
. . . .

TRADING UP (aka The Jennifer Garner Approach)

As you move along through the dating world, we suggest that you upgrade whenever possible. We call this the Jennifer Garner Approach. Sure, she was a star on a hit show, but she was pretty much stuck on the B-list famewise because her show was a genre show and her husband was Scott Foley. Scott Foley seems like a swell guy to us, but let's all agree that being Mrs. Scott Foley isn't going to get you on the cover of *Us Weekly* anytime soon. So what do you do? Upgrade, baby! As usual, the easiest place to look when looking for a potential upgrade (and really, this is where it becomes the Angelina Jolie Approach), is your costars. Preferably, go for the hottest one available to you. Jennifer Garner nailed this perfectly by upgrading to her super hot costar Michael Vartan. Now THAT'S how you get a cover! Dumping your current squeeze for the more attractive version is a pretty American thing to do. You just have to be careful to make sure you move on to someone your audience approves of. People loved Garner and Vartan as a couple on *Alias*, so they were pretty accepting of them as a couple in real life. But Jen wasn't done with climbing the relationship ladder yet! She made her final upgrade when she landed a true A-lister in Ben Affleck. Ben was fresh off the Bennifer disaster, people were REALLY rooting for him to settle down with a nice girl, and Jennifer Garner fit the mold. They got to live happily ever after, and both of them remain cemented into the A-list for life. Everybody won!

Now, Jennifer Garner's exploits take us to relationship territory, something that we know an awful lot about. Bottom line, getting into a celebrity relationship is a good thing. America wants people to pair up. We root for it. We love to criticize bad relationships. We even give tax breaks to married couples. Seriously, in this country, the government actually PAYS you to get married! Being in a couple makes you more relatable and human. It gives something extra in your life for people to cheer for or against. Clearly, we're all about pairing up. The benefits of being in a celebrity relationship are huge.

LEAN ON ME

· ·

Additionally, it takes a bit of the pressure off of you to always have to be ON. Maybe there are times in your life and career (and when you're a celebrity, they're sort of the same thing, right?) when you don't have quite as much going on as you'd like. Well, if there are TWO of you, you've got twice as many chances to get covered, right? It's definitely nice to have someone to go through it all with, but at the same time it doesn't hurt to be able to ride your partner's coattails from time to time (as long as it goes both ways, of course). Of course, being in a couple can often BE what you have going on in your lives. Maybe there's no movie to promote or show that's premiering or fashion line to debut right now, but there is ALWAYS a relationship update to be given. Being in a celebrity couple is a constant source of media interest, which, of course, is a very good thing.

> **At the end of the day, make choices like you would in any other romantic situation.**

Obviously, no one has benefited more from these equations than we have, which should tell you a couple of things. One, make sure you're not boring or no one will pay attention to you; two, being in a celebrity couple opens doors. Do you think either of us would be where we are today without the other person? It goes without saying that we wouldn't be. We reiterate: Speidi > Heidi + Spencer. This, of course, leads us to the most important thing to remember when pairing up in a celebrity couple, which is: make sure you're really into the person. Sure, we do well by being a couple, but if we weren't as in love as we are, it wouldn't be worth it. At the end of the day, make choices like you would in any other romantic situation. Being in a celebrity couple is just like being in a regular couple in that way, only we get to be on magazine covers and host cool parties!

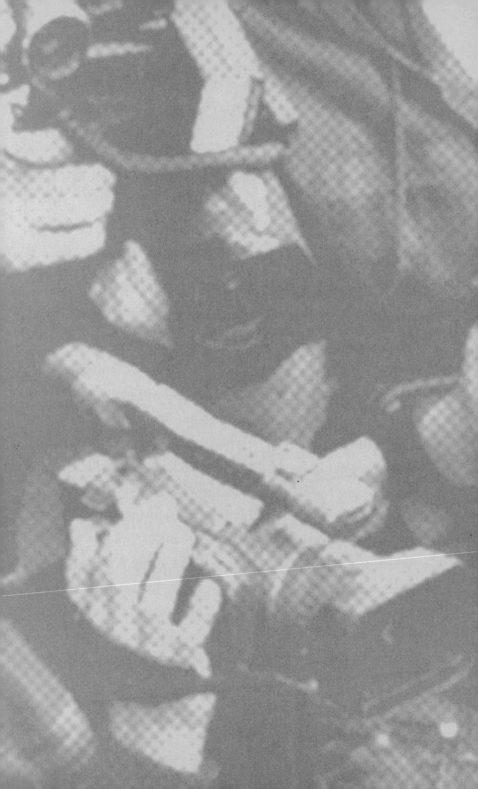

8

★ BUILDING YOUR BRAND

Perhaps nothing is more important in maintaining your celebrity status than having a recognizable brand. It's the next level beyond creating your character. Just playing a role is one thing. Spinning that role into multiple ventures requires a tremendous amount of energy, so be prepared. Being one-dimensional can take you only so far, though. If you're a one-trick pony, your show is very short, isn't it? So you need to diversify, and in order to do that, you need to have a brand that people know.

Most people think of branding as something that's just for companies. When people say "brand," you think Nabisco or Coke or Cadillac. But here's the important thing. When we say Nabisco, you think cookies, right? And then you think, man, I could really go for an Oreo right about now. And you know what? You're gonna go buy an Oreo now. It's too late. It's in your head. You can't help it now, and you're just gonna sit there and think about it until you satisfy your craving and go get an Oreo. That's the power of branding. When you have something so recognizable that it leads people's thoughts right to your product, you're going to be very successful. And that should be your goal as a celebrity. You want people to think of you and instantly connect you with something that is going to lead to you making money. You know, because actually working sucks.

For example, if you're someone that's famous for . . . well, for being famous, it's probably going to be a lot easier for you to write and sell a book about how to get famous now, isn't it? And that's the key. Once your brand is established people will PAY YOU just to be you in one capacity

or another. Pretty great, right? For us, it was fairly simple. Our characters are the hot, blond troublemakers who will stab you in the back but do it with a smile. We're also completely over-the-top and out there in our nonshow lives, and we make sure that extends into everything we do. That's why when you see all of those pap pics of us, we always participate and play along. It's all about pounding the idea of who you are into people's heads so when someone is looking for something specific you come to mind. Because we've been so aware of doing that, you can't avoid us even if you want to. Turn on *Ugly Betty*? There we are! At a club in Vegas? We're the guests of honor! Looking for some hip clothes on Robertson? Why not stop into Kitson and pick up some Heidiwood! The best way to STAY famous is to find your way into multiple ventures in multiple media, and the best way to do that is to have an easily recognizable brand.

> **Take things about yourself that people may not know and run with them.**

Remember that brand building requires you to go out into territories that you may not be naturally familiar with. But if you want your empire to grow, you must branch out. We're not saying change up your character because you don't want to alienate your current followers. But take things about yourself that people may not know and run with them. It can only help. Case in point: in the middle of the last election, John McCain had the Republican nomination wrapped up early while Obama and Hillary were still duking it out. NO ONE was talking about McCain. Well, almost no one. Heidi, a lifelong Re-

publican, made it known who she was supporting. She even had a public lunch with McCain's daughter, Meghan.

What happened? McCain spent the next two days saying Heidi's name over and over again in public as every pundit he talked to asked him about Heidi's endorsement. He even called her "a very talented actress"! Just to recap: in the middle of the most historic election in the history of the country, HEIDI MONTAG became part of the national discussion. Let's say that again. John Freakin' McCain talked about Heidi on TV for two straight days! A few more percentage points in the other direction and we would have been dining at the White House and sleeping in the Lincoln Bedroom, people. The bottom line is this. Be recognizable, and be out there, EVERYWHERE, as much as you can, and things will start coming to you instead of the other way around.

The most successful example ever of a person brand building has got to be Donald Trump. People get famous for all kinds of things. But if you started at the top of the

> **Having people repeat your name over and over is a great way to build a brand.**

list of reasons why it happens, where would *real estate developer* be? Don't you start with *actor, rock star, athlete,* and *politician,* and then move your way to *reality star* and then down to even *socialite* and below? But Trump went from renovating a single hotel to having a star on the Hollywood Walk of Fame! How did this happen? The first thing we all can learn from the Donald is that you should absolutely put your name on everything. The man has dozens of hotels named after him all over the world. It's brilliant. People like hotels. People stay in hotels all the time. When someone asks you where you stayed and your answer is someone's NAME, that person is doing something very smart. Having people repeat your name over and over is a great way to build a brand. Give them a reason to.

His greatest stroke of genius, though, was parlaying all of this into what was, for a while, the biggest show on television. Trump was smart enough to see the trend toward reality TV and make a move in that direction when he produced and starred on *The Apprentice*. But NO ONE would have given him a show if he didn't carry with him the Trump brand. How easy a pitch must THAT have been? "I'm a famous guy with a brand that everyone knows means success in business. I'm also completely over-the-top with everything I say. Give me a show where I teach people to be and act like me and every week I fire someone for being a loser." That must have been the shortest meeting in the history of television. What else could a network say other than, uh, yes. Can you please start tomorrow so we can begin printing money?! But again, without building his brand, he's just another real estate developer who no one has ever heard of. Not that that's a bad thing. If you want to learn how to be one of those, buy one of the dozen books Trump's been paid to write on the subject.

Hmm. Writing a book about the thing you're most known for. What a great way to build a brand!

9

GETTING WORK DONE IS YOUR JOB, BY HEIDI

Whatever women need to do to feel sexy, they should do.

—HEIDI MONTAG

And that's the truth. There was a time when having a little work done was considered taboo. At least that's what I've heard. The fact is that in this day and age, the list of celebrities who HAVEN'T had work done is shorter than the list of those who have. Boobs, butts, noses, lips, foreheads, stomachs . . . you name it, it can be upgraded.

And really, why not? I can't for the life of me think of a single reason why a person shouldn't be able to look exactly the way they want to. Sure, there are healthier ways to lose weight than stapling your stomach, but you can't diet or exercise your way into bigger boobs or a smaller nose.

> *I believe in the judicious use of plastic surgery.*
> **—COURTENEY COX**

As a celebrity, you're constantly going to be judged by how you look. That's just how it is. It's your JOB to look good, the same way it's a fireman's job to put out fires and it's a policeman's job to fight crime. Magazine editors zoom in on every picture they look at to the point where their entire screens are filled with just one spot on your thigh or stomach. And don't even get me started on being on TV in the age of HD. But if you don't want people looking at you in that way, work at a bank. Otherwise, you need to present yourself well at all times. Of course, fashion and exercise play a part, and I obviously recognize the importance of all that.

> *Plastic surgeons are always making mountains out of mole hills.*
> **—DOLLY PARTON**

But if you don't wake up in the morning and get out of the shower loving what you see, it's going to be a lot harder projecting confidence, which is key to being a star.

Before I go on, let me say two things: (1) I'm not saying plastic surgery is necessarily for everyone. If you're 100 percent confident in how you look and don't feel the need to change a single thing that you can't do on your own, more power to you. (2) Don't kid yourself. Nobody's born perfect, but you CAN get there if you want by working hard at it and letting the beauty of modern science handle the rest. The upside here is limitless. Not only will you look better and feel better about yourself, there is no better way to get instant attention than to completely change your look.

Before we get into some specifics, the last thing I want to say is that after you do it and feel fully recovered, you should absolutely, 100 percent talk about it. My recommendation is to wait a couple of weeks and make one or two appearances before you say anything, just to get people talking about it. The key to getting the biggest publicity push on it is to tease the story by being seen, let the story build up through speculation, then give the interview. It's key to wait long enough to allow the story to grow, but to not wait *too* long for either the story to die or for people to have seen your new body so many times that it's not a revelation anymore.

> **Nobody's born perfect, but you CAN get there.**

After I had my surgery, I was photographed walking on the beach with Spencer; the pictures ran in *Us Weekly*, and EVERYONE was talking about it! Sure, I wasn't shy about showing off my body. I never am. But all they had at first were some paparazzi pictures of me walking on the beach.

> **I waited another week before talking about it to allow the buzz to spread.**

You could see the difference, of course, but I waited another week before talking about it to allow the buzz to spread. And you know what? That's how I got my first *Us Weekly* cover. What's amazing to me now is that I was actually kind of scared and reluctant to talk about it at the time. I was worried about just being the plastic-surgery girl. But it ended up being the best decision of my career because once I talked about it, there was no speculation anymore. It was all just out there. Usually, I wouldn't suggest putting an end to a story line, but if it ends up on a magazine cover, you've done your job. Don't worry, keep reading and you'll find plenty more ways to create buzz!

Let's get into some specifics now. There are SO many options out there these days, and I want to go over them for you:

▶ BOOBS

Let's face it, we all love boobs. Men love them, women love them, gay men love them . . . what's not to love? There is no surgery you can get that will get you more instant attention, and you know why? Because people are ALREADY staring at your boobs!

It's just a fact of life. So when they change size, people notice it right away. To me, the key is to go big enough that there's a noticeable difference, but not so big that you look

like a cartoon character—one to two sizes max. I was an A/small B cup and went up to a full C. Just big enough to get noticed, but not over-the-top.

If you want to go extreme here, there's always the option of taking them out and, for that matter, putting them back in again. Pamela Anderson made a career out of this (well, this and taping herself having sex with rock stars, but that's another chapter, perhaps another book). She had them taken out and put back in more times than I can count. It was like changing a sweater to her. But you know what? Every time she did it, people noticed. There's a reason that she's one of the most recognizable women in the world, and it's not because of her fine work in *Barb Wire*.

► NOSE

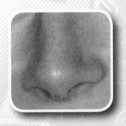

Repeat after me: *deviated septum*. Put this on the short list of words you must know, along with *exhaustion*. Seriously, it's like those analogies on the SATs. Deviated septum is to nose job as exhaustion is to rehab. In reality, a deviated septum is either a freak condition you're born with or the result of getting your nose smashed. It happens to boxers. The weird thing is, a freakish number of celebrities just HAPPEN to have been born with one. Tragic, right? Anyway, do whatever you want to your nose. All you have to do is blame it on the fact that you just couldn't breathe. Afterward, you can go on and on how you've never felt better, how you've never gotten such a great night's sleep. You don't even snore anymore! You get what I'm saying. This is without question the easiest surgery to explain away, and since we're talking about the dead center of your face, you can get a huge upgrade with little to no negative reaction. Cameron Diaz and Jennifer Aniston both did it; take a look at earlier pictures of them. Huge upgrades. Unless you're going for a VERY specific look, you definitely want to have a nose that doesn't dominate your face, and they both look a thousand times better for it. Ashlee Simpson is another person who talked about it and she went from being the "other" Simpson girl to being hotter than her sister! Bottom line, there are very few people I've ever met that couldn't use an upgrade on their schnoz. Embrace it!

▶ BOTOX

My favorite line about Botox came from *American Idol*'s Simon Cowell. He said, "To me, Botox is no more unusual than toothpaste. It works. You do it once a year. Who cares?" The weird thing about that is that it implies that he only brushes his teeth once a year, doesn't it? Anyway, I've never done it, but it seems to me like a bad idea disguised as a good one. Everything I've ever heard says that it makes it impossible for you to have different facial expressions. How are you going to show people you hate them if you can't show emotion? Anything that inhibits your ability to be in a feud is a bad thing, as far as I'm concerned. Bottom line, it's an old person's procedure. If you're at the point where you need Botox, you better have mastered everything in this book YEARS ago, or it's just too late.

▶ LIPS

At this point, getting your lips injected is no different than getting your nails done or wearing a push-up bra. You can test it for a couple of weeks, and if you don't like it, everything goes back to normal. Again, this is great for a sudden burst of attention, but even better, you don't HAVE to live with it for life. If it goes wrong, you can just let it wear off, and it gives you the possibility of going up and 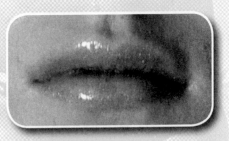 down without having to go under the knife a la Pam with her boobs! EVERYBODY does this one. Paris Hilton, Jessica Simpson, and yours truly, to name a few.

▶ BUTT

This is a nutty one. There has been all kinds of speculation on whether or not Kim Kardashian had them, and it doesn't even matter whether or not she did. The questions have given her the most famous butt since J. Lo and that's a great thing. Be careful on this one. Lots of celebs like Kim cry ethnicity as the reason for having a bunch of junk in the trunk. If you're a little white girl from Colorado like me, it's gonna be tough to pull this one off without people calling you out. Personally, I'd go boobs over the butt. Don't underestimate the importance of things being at eye level, you know?

▶ TEETH

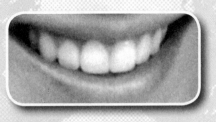

I'm all for this one. Caps are key. There's nothing more important than your smile (well, except your boobs, of course), and the brighter and whiter the better. It draws people into your face, which—assuming you've taken care of everything else on this list—should be a good thing!

▶ FACE-LIFTS, ETC.

See *Botox*. This is for old people. Maybe we'll put out a senior-citizen edition of this book one day, but for now, enjoy your youthful face!

10

FAMOUSLY EVER AFTER

Some people might tell you that your wedding is a private moment that should only be shared with family and close friends. That's fine for civilians. But if you want to maintain your fame and keep people interested, you must invite the public to all of your most intimate occasions, and your wedding is at the top of the list. That's why you must make sure it gets into a magazine. When it comes to weddings, you're pretty much guaranteed an appearance on the cover.

Think about it. Avril Lavigne, Fergie, Jeff Gordon, Tori Spelling. Are these people that you'd normally associate with being on the cover of a tabloid? Well guess what landed them on covers? You got it: their weddings. It's just like celebrity math. It doesn't matter what list you're on, if it's your wedding day and you're even remotely famous, you're gonna snag that cover story.

The best part about your wedding being in print is that you have control over how you're covered in a way you won't ever have again (until you have babies, that is). You have control over what pictures can be used, who they can and can't talk to, and the overall tone of the story, since you're more than likely giving an interview to go along with the pictures. You're going to be portrayed in a positive light. Every woman looks great in her wedding dress (and you're going to be able to afford a really nice one thanks to the money you're making off of selling the pictures!). You're going to fill a magazine's pages with tons of "Aww . . ." moments, and that can only be a good thing. Women especially love a wedding, and the majority of people who read the tabloids are women. Remember, your wedding day is the one moment in your life where it's completely OK, even EXPECTED that everything is about you. As a celebrity, you're living your whole life like that, so you might as well make the most of this opportunity to look good!

> **Women especially love a wedding, and the majority of people who read the tabloids are women.**

You don't have to look any further than us to see how a wedding (or weddings) work to your benefit. As we've discussed already, we haven't exactly been the most loved couple over the years. But everything changed for us after our first wedding in Cabo.

When people saw just how obviously in love we were, they couldn't help but feel better about us. A wedding, even a quickie elopement on vacation, like ours was, legitimizes a relationship in a way nothing else can, and people respond positively to that. We used to walk down the street and some people would actually yell at us because they believed the way we were portrayed on TV really showed everything there was to

A wedding is also huge news.

know about us. But after we got married people had nothing but great things to say to us. We went skiing and people were yelling out well wishes as we went down the mountain! It was crazy!

A wedding is also huge news. Around the time we got married the first time, things had been a bit slow for us news-wise. The show was on a break and things were way too calm in our personal lives to make headlines. We love going to Cabo, and when the idea struck Spencer that we should just be spontaneous, we didn't hesitate. Sure, there were a million things running through our heads at the time from our parents' reactions to the people on our show not being around.

But one thing that we didn't worry about was whether or not anyone would be paying attention when the news came out. Of course, it blew up. We were on the cover of *Us Weekly*, and every mag and website out there was talking about whether or not it was "real" or not. It was the smartest move we ever made. Well, maybe the second smartest.

After all of the fallout from the first wedding (including a second *Us* cover story, in which Heidi's mom went ballistic on us), we realized that this whole "it wasn't a real wedding" story had legs. Well, who are we to blow against the wind? So what do you do then? Have ANOTHER wedding, of course!

This time we did it up right. Did we have the chance to keep it secure and sell the wedding pictures to a magazine for a huge payday? OF COURSE we did! But we're the authors of *How to Be Famous*, not *How to Make a Quick Buck*. We went for it, fully on camera, in a church, with our families, friends, costars, media, etc. It was a total celebration of all things Speidi, and everyone was invited. We even put the pictures out to every single website and magazine that wanted them. The result? We were on FIVE magazine covers that week. Sure, there were other things going on, but nobody bought a magazine that week without flipping through pages and pages of our big day. And that's the goal, right?

Of course, the other effect the second wedding had was that we completely took over a show that we were meant to

just be a secondary part of. That sealed our nemesis' fate, as she left for good. As you sit here reading this book, we're now the central focus of our show, having completed that first journey from afterthought to centerpiece. THAT'S how to be famous, people.

EPILOGUE

Congrats, you've reached the end. If you've followed our advice, by now you should have an assistant reading you this chapter while you lounge by the pool at a five-star hotel (or in rehab . . . no difference, right?).

All we can say to you at this point is don't get lazy. Fame is a fickle thing, and you have to treat it differently than you would a regular day job. If you're a teacher, you eventually get tenured and you can just sail along for the rest of your career. If you work in an office, you'll get health care and a 401(k), so you'll be taken care of in your old age. But there's no pension plan for celebrities, so don't ever stop working it.

Sure, you're famous now, but one dry spell and you can fall off the map for good. You should be grateful for every day you're alive on this planet and doubly so if you're famous. We may not be saving the world here . . .

. . . or are we? Wait a minute. When did being entertained and therefore happy become a luxury? Isn't it part of the Declaration of Independence? "Life, liberty, and the pursuit of happiness"? Isn't bringing fun, laughter, and feuds into someone's life the best thing people could possibly do for others? Maybe celebrities ARE important! Take this newfound responsibility as an honor. Your audience is depending on you!

In Case of Emergency

*I*f all else fails to get you noticed, here are some last-ditch strategies:

1. Become beloved star-athlete. Kill wife. Get away with it.
2. If you're a man, get pregnant.
3. Become the leader of a cult.
4. Get shot in the face by the vice president.
5. Be really unqualified. Get selected as presidential running mate.
6. Get your leg blown off. Marry famous rock star. Divorce him.
7. If you're a prostitute: Have sex with a governor.
8. Become Olympic skater. Have your rival's legs broken.
9. Become Olympic skater. Have your legs broken by your rival.
10. Land a plane in the Hudson River saving everyone on board.
11. Have six kids. Then have eight more—all at once.
12. Become hated reality TV stars. Write book on fame.